To Rhyme or Not to Rhyme...

MESSAGES

of the Heart

Whether you are happy in love, hurting in love, separated from the one you love, presently losing or have recently lost someone you love, confused about when to let go, or even if you are happily single... this book has a message for you.

AnGenette D. Jackson

authorHOUSE®

AuthorHouse™
1663 Liberty Drive, Suite 200
Bloomington, IN 47403
www.authorhouse.com
Phone: 1-800-839-8640

First published by AuthorHouse 5/27/2008

ISBN: 978-1-4343-7856-9 (sc)

Library of Congress Control Number: 2008903421

Printed in the United States of America
Bloomington, Indiana

This book is printed on acid-free paper.

Inspirations

Cassandra—1999 (Former coworker—Wachovia Bank Card Fraud Prevention Dept.)

After I had written my first poem, I shared it with my co-workers. I was surprised that they really liked it. A few days later, Cassandra came up to me and said, "A.J. have you written any more poems lately?" Her question halted me. She had no idea how difficult writing that first poem was. I began to experience feelings of inadequacy. I have always and ever shall be my biggest critic, so when someone else points out something that I should or could have done, I get extremely bothered. I thought to myself: Do you think poems flow out of me as easily as the water flows downstream? But Cassandra made me think…maybe I should make an effort to write more poems.

Thanks Cassandra.

Simon—2005 (Former colleague and mentor—Lithonia Middle School)

We were sitting in one of the many mandatory teacher training sessions that often occupied so much of our valuable time, when Simon and I were talking. She said to me, "Lucas you have a book in you, and someday you're going to write it."

Thanks Simon.

Team 7B students at R. L. Clements Middle School—2006-2007

Your talent served as the catalyst I needed. Thanks for the opportunity to teach and learn from you!

Keisha Porter—2007 (my TRU'S desk partner at Bellsouth 2000-2005)

When I first decided to temporarily move back to my hometown, depression began to set in. I ran into my TRU'S co-worker at the post office in Lithonia, and told her that maybe it was time for me to explore this venture. Keisha said, "A.J. writing a book is a fabulous idea!" People never know how powerful a few encouraging words can be.

Thanks Keisha.

Spikes (Blue)—2007 (my friend of inspiration)

After deciding to take a sabbatical, I met my friend Spikes. Ours was a friendship that quickly blossomed. During one of our extensive discussions on the topic of lifetime goals and passions, I told him that I enjoyed writing. He asked to hear a sample. After I shared a few poems with him he said, "A.J. you need to do something with those words." Spikes continued to listen to my efforts and offer encouragement.

Thank you Spikes for being so <u>influential</u> in my life.

Special thanks to Alan L. Sherman (author of "Lessons Learned for Lessons Lived") for your advice, encouragement, and support, and to M.F.T. for keeping me company, listening to me gripe, and always trying to make me laugh as the treatment for my ulcer!

A.J.

Acknowledgements

My life may have taken a different path if not for the decisions made by the following people:

J. Dees (Manager) and A. Bowser (Asst. H. R. Director) at an Alabama bank:

I'm glad you didn't hire me. Working full-time would not have allotted me the time required to complete this project. Thanks for noticing that I was destined for more than hitting your clock from eight to four!

Alabama State Department of Education:

Thanks for having such a frustrating process for teachers from different states to obtain licensure due to the highly qualified guidelines. Had I been granted a teaching certificate when I first relocated, I certainly would not have had the time, inspiration, motivation, or energy to focus on this project.

Dr. Flint (College Advisor):

Thanks for rejecting the portfolio I submitted. Obtaining the certification may have dissuaded me from relinquishing my teaching position to take a hiatus, and relocating to complete this project.

None of you will ever know how much your rejections have meant to me!

To everyone out there who has ever been rejected, "Never give up! Your success awaits you."

Dedication

Thanks to all of my family and friends

for putting up with me throughout my madness!

Contents

Oh how wonderful
newfound love is

Incessantly a beautiful
melody plays

I'm told that this is the
dancing phase

Enjoy it while it lasts

Precious Moments

I smile when I think of you
My mind consumed with reflections
Of moments we've spent together
When you make me laugh
Or when we sit in silence
It matters not where we are
As long as we're together

Like the day we first met
How we shared one lunch
Because you were low on funds
The agreement we made
To be open and honest with each other always

Like when we went to your friend's house
So you could show me how to shoot pool
Our bodies innocently touching
Yet the chemistry was undeniable

Like our daily conversations
Until the wee hours in the morning
How I have to tell you to wake up
Because you'd rather fall asleep talking
Than hang up the telephone
Seems we're addicted to each other's voices

Like the day I came over
And we watched television
While snuggling on the sofa
How I enjoyed just being with you

Like the first time you hugged me
Or half hugged me
And I had to ask you to hold me tighter
Now you have mastered the art of hugging me

Like that time when you were following me
All the way out the door on my way to work
As I walked, I kept stopping
And we kissed over and over again
Two lovers who didn't want to part ways

Like our intimate encounters
And the way we spoon all night afterwards
You make me feel so safe

So many pleasant thoughts
Of precious moments we've spent together
Overshadow all of the differences we've had
Precious moments make me smile
When I think of you

When I Think of You

There are times
When I think of you
And I wonder
What you're doing at that very moment
How you're feeling
If you're thinking of me, too
If you're longing for me
As intensely
As I'm longing for you
If you're even aware of how often
I experience this overpowering desire
To spend my every waking moment with you
Lying on your chest
Or in your lap
Or closely tucked behind you in bed
As long as we're touching
Skin to skin
In the most relaxing state I've ever been
Never wanting this time to end
With the obliteration of outside factors
Nothing else seems to matter
Is it selfish of me
To want this to be
My life eternally
There are times
When it appears too good to be true
I only feel this way
When I think of you

What I See

You gave me a new start
Like jumper cables
Connected to the terminals of a dead battery

You recognized that
My desire was trapped in a burning building
Your entrance calmed the raging fires within because
You offered safety

You invited me to be free from the shackles of shame
Those that result from the egregious acts of violation

You proved to me that
Not all come to manipulate and deceive
But some come to restore and relieve

You showed me hope
That joy may actually exist down the road for me
Yes hope
When I look at you
That's what I see

My Desire

It's time for another encounter

My walls are jumping

Excited with the anticipation of receiving you

Reflecting on the magic of your touch

It's you that I want

Come to me

I need you to

Come inside of me

Now

When You Love Someone

When you love someone
You can't explain why
Though you could list many undesirable attributes
To describe that someone
And if placed on a scale
The bowl holding them would be full
So full that the scale mirrors an unbalanced seesaw
With someone sitting only on one side
While on the other side of the scale
You see through the crystal bowl
As if it's empty
Because you can't fill it with reasons
Why you love that someone
You just do

Friends and family members often magnify the flaws
In the bowl on the left side of the scale
And in their opinions you have no justification
For loving that someone
But in your mind your behavior is justified
You love that someone
Just because you do

It's not any particular act that's performed
Nor any specific word that's spoken
And it isn't how attractive that someone may be
It's as if your spirit is being drawn by a magnet
Causing you to find that someone irresistibly appealing
No matter how inexplicable it seems
You love that someone
With everything that's inside of you
It's undeniable
And it's evident in your every move
Continuously giving of yourself
Sacrificing your wants and needs
And you do it because seeing that someone happy
Makes you happy
Because when you love someone
You show it in everything you do

Falling Asleep With Him

He stands 6'3" in stature with broad shoulders
His feet extend just off the edge of my bed
He's always said that my bed was too short for him
"Loosen the flat sheet so that I can stretch out," he bellows.
After lying down he turns his back to me

"Hold me," I whisper in a whining voice.
"Woman I'm tired!
Don't you know I worked twelve hours today?" he says.
Then he willingly turns on his back
I bury my head in his chest and gently stroke it
He maneuvers his arm from beneath me
To join it with the other one
As if he's hugging me
The warmness I feel from his touch is immeasurable
We converse briefly in a soft tone
Until a silence falls on the room
I lie in his arms
More content than I feel at any other time during the day
We begin to read one another's minds
I feel satisfied with the amount of time he's held me
He feels as if he's held me long enough
At the same instant we both begin to speak
"OK, turn back over so you can get some rest," I say.
"Let me turn over so that I can get some sleep," he says.
Again he has his back to me
"Come close to me," he says in a soft voice.
I tuck myself behind him so close

It is as if we are one
If I could, I would consume him
So that he would be contained within me
With our souls forever intertwined

I put my arm over him
He grabs and holds it between his arms
I'm holding him from behind
But I feel as though he's holding me
The feeling of this level of security
Surpasses any installed electronic device
My psyche exudes peacefulness
As I think to myself…
'Oh how I love this man'
Before falling asleep with him

When You Show That You Want Me

When you show that you want me
My insides contract
And expand
Contract and expand
Like an accordion
Being played by a musician
As the bellows go in and out
Beautiful music is made
You are the musician
I am the only one who hears your music
When you show that you want me

When you show that you want me
That middle school feeling of butterflies
In my stomach arrives
I welcome it
Taking me back in time
When I had no pressing cares or concerns
Now you take care of me
And all of my cares and concerns
When you show that you want me

When you show that you want me
Nothing else matters
Not how much money I owe
No deadlines that need to be met
No appointments that need to be kept
None that need to be set
When you show that you want me

My only appointment is with you
When I know that you want me

As You Sit Across the Room

If I could only read your mind
Those times I wonder what you're thinking
What type of thoughts would I find
As you sit across the room from me

From time to time I stare at you
Amazed by your beauty
Whether you're reading or writing
Working on the computer
Watching television
Folding laundry or cooking
It matters not what you're doing

This is true quality time
I just want you with me
In the same space
At the same moment
So I can just look at you

I'm on an emotional high
When you look up
And we catch each other's eyes
The look of love is on your face
That's all I need to see
As you sit across the room from me

I Vanish When You Appear

Like an out of body experience I watch myself
Or someone who looks like me
Her physical traits are identical
But I don't recognize her actions
She's behaving so out of character
According to what I see
I can't believe that she is me

She doesn't show up
Until you appear
And upon your arrival I disappear

I refuse to accept that she is me
Catering to you so selflessly
Performing acts I'd never do
Who is this woman submitting herself to you

Should I be envious
Or appreciative
As I watch you smile at her
The smile that once belonged solely to me
You leave the room
She instantly vanishes in the air
As if she were never there
I find myself alone waiting for you to return

At that moment I understand
When you come around
I am the woman that you need me to be
I can supply all of your needs
Because you complete me
Now I can see
That she is me

Precious Moments Part 2

Just when I thought I could handle no more
You had other precious moments in store
You make me feel so special when I'm with you
I can't explain why I feel this way
I just do

Like the night you had a few dollars
So we went to Tasty for a couple of dinners
This time we didn't have to share
I enjoyed feeding you and being fed
I didn't even mind you whipping me into embarrassment
In Ms. Pac-Man and Galaga

Like the night we took a bath together
Soaking in the tub by candlelight
Listening to the soothing sounds of Anita
You jokingly accused me of violating you with the washcloth
Oh how I hoped for many more of those nights

Like the other day when I came over to watch television
We watched Hunter or Hunted
While snuggling on the sofa
Nothing and no one else mattered at that time

Like the way we spent New Year's Eve
Unraveling my double strand twists
While watching 'National Treasure'
You struggled at first
But soon bragged about how good you were
Once you got the hang of it
Exactly at midnight
We shared a kiss that seemed magical

Like the morning we had breakfast
While completing your online job application
You raved about how good the biscuits were
Before I left for work, I gave you my last bite
Then you asked me where your hug was
It made my heart smile to know
That my hugs make you feel as good
As your hugs make me feel

Like the night we watched the comedy show
While I redid my double strand twists
You wrapped your arms around my waist for hours
Holding on tightly until you fell asleep
Your gentle snoring was melodic

Like the night you were sitting up watching television
As I was lying on my back relaxing
You moved to lie on my left
Propped up on your elbows
Held out the remote
And told me I could choose what we watched
I couldn't believe it
The television addict was relinquishing control
I turned to move in closer with you looking down at me
Told you I didn't care what we watched
I only wanted to lie there next to you

Over and over again
My face
Became the dark, rich soil
Your tender kisses
Became the beautiful, peach gladiolas
You gently planted

Soon neither of us cared what was on the television
Because it was watching us

You have been a welcome presence in my life
I will always treasure the time we spend together
I only wish our precious moments could last forever

Sometimes good, sometimes bad

Some we wish we never had

All together each played a part

In designing our personalities

And shaping our hearts

LIFE

EXPERIENCES

Parents Have Feelings, Too

It was my 12th birthday
Mommie had just picked me up from school
The car packed with balloons
Every year I wanted the same thing
Lots of balloons and a yellow cake with cream cheese icing
This year would be different though
I had an unusual request
Then the question was posed
What did I want as a gift
How could I tell her
How would she respond
The lead in my chest grew heavier by the second
My inner voice advised me to spit out the words
And then they were out there
Piercing the air like pins popping my balloons
Those irretrievable words
My gift of choice
To live with my grandmother
Mommie ranted and raved so loudly
How could I be ignorant of her pain
What a shock it must be to learn that
The child you made so many sacrifices for
Doesn't want to live with you anymore
Where did you go wrong
What could you have done differently
Why you
I learned that parents have feelings, too
Wow
Parents have feelings, too

My Antipathy

I couldn't do anything without you
I couldn't go anywhere without you
Why did you come here
Couldn't you have gone somewhere else
Bothered someone else
Forced to give up my teenage years
And for what
To cook and clean
Bath and dress
Chauffer and baby sit
All because of you
I wished you wouldn't have come here
I wished I could have left
To go somewhere else
Anywhere
So I wouldn't have had to give up my adolescence

Because of you
My pessimism grew
Enraged with resentment
I mistreated you
Misplaced anger confused me
My eyes were so clouded I couldn't see
That it wasn't your fault
You didn't ask to come here
Anymore than me
So why were we brought here

I hope you can forgive me
What a horrible sister I've been
You needed me to be your friend
You should have been enjoying your childhood
Totally carefree
Instead I was being as mean as I could be
I hope you can accept my apology

I never want to bring a child into this place
To be inflicted with my unhappiness
Does that make me a disgrace

A Mind Too Young

I was 13
With a mind too young
To be immersed in such a topic
But she didn't care
Wasn't she the one responsible for protecting me
Weren't my needs to be placed before hers
Didn't she know how deeply she could hurt me
If she knew
She didn't care
Without hesitation she said it
Her words
Were like blades trimming the little happiness I felt
From the deepest chambers of my heart
Just as fat is removed from lean meat and discarded
I didn't think my pathetic life could get any worse
Than at that very moment
I had just finished cleaning the kitchen
And sat down to the dining room table to talk to her
Then she spoke
So casually
As if she were asking
If I wanted hamburgers for dinner the next day
How do you answer someone when they ask you
If you want a new dad
I never considered replacing my dad
The one person in the world
Who seemed to show me some love
Why take him away

What would I have left

With no one else to love me

Why would I want to keep living

Why would you deliberately hurt someone that you love

Did she love me

I wasn't sure

But I was sure that

I was 13

With a mind too young

In Her Quiet Way

In the morning...
She looks at me and frowns
Then she sighs before speaking in a hushed tone
You need just a little more material on that skirt
And I know what she's saying
PUT ON SOME CLOTHES
WALKING 'ROUND HERE HALF-NAKED
LIKE YOU CRAZY OR SUMTHIN'
She is my well-learned grandmother
In her wisdom telling me what's best for her granddaughter

In the afternoon...
I walk into the kitchen
She's sitting at the table patiently perusing a pamphlet
And I know what she's saying
I'M HUNGRY
WHATCHU TRYIN' TO DO STARVE ME TO DEATH
FIX ME SUMTHIN' T'EAT NOW GIRL
She is my witty grandmother
The guardian who tells me what to do in her sarcastic way

In the evening...
She stays at the table until I come back into the kitchen
She points at my daddie's plate and at her plate
And I know what she's saying
YOUR DADDY IS WASTING FOOD
AND HE DON'T 'PRECIATE YOUR HARD WORK
BUT I ATE ALL OF MINE
She is my slightly demented grandmother
Reverting back to a stage of childhood

Telling on her friend for not eating all of his vegetables

In the night time…
She walks into the room we share
To put on her night clothes
I'm listening to music and talking on the telephone
She looks at me after she finishes changing
And I know what she's saying
YOU GON' HAFTA GET OUTTA HERE
MAKIN' ALL THAT FUSS
I'M GOING TO BED NOW
She is my decisive grandmother
The matriarch who believes that everyone must go to bed
At the same time that she goes every day
And I love when she speaks to me in her quiet way

Cursed With Two Faces

She was unusually mean to me
And I couldn't figure out why

A laundry list of chores
Extra responsibilities
Forced to sacrifice my freedom
To care for siblings whose existence I loathed
Why was she so mean to me
Across the world
That's where she said she wanted to send me
On a ship that would never come back
If years ago there was readily available contraception
For me there would never have been a conception
That's what she told me
You're just like your low down daddy
That's what she said
So it was clear
When she looked at me, she saw his face
And all the heartaches and disappointments
She'd experienced since they met
If she could wish me away she would have, I bet

He was unusually demanding of me
And I couldn't figure out why

Sixteen times a day or more he called my name
Come do this
Go do that

This is not good enough

No that's wrong

His voice began to cause my ulcer to flare up

Because he was so critical

But he loved me

That's what he said

He didn't know why he acted like he did

That's what he told me

You act just like your mama

You sound and look like her, too

So it was clear

When he looked at me

He saw her face

And all the heartaches and disappointments

He'd experienced since they met

So now I fret

Because I'm cursed with two faces

It Starts With One Word

It starts with one word
The one that never should have been spoken
One unsatisfactory word to
Disappoint
Discourage
Dispel one's contented state of mind
Destroy harmony
Damage relationships
Disturb a peaceful environment
Voices escalate
Tempers flare
A word in the air
Irrevocable once there
Why is it that people can be so cruel
Deliberately using spoken word as a weapon
An unnecessary tool
Often yielding unexpected repercussions
Consequences that could have been avoided
If only someone had swallowed that one word
And chosen to listen instead of speak
One word
Before you speak…THINK

Stages of Life

You were my hero
When I was an infant
In my blissful state of ignorance
You could do no wrong
And I loved you

As a child the blindfold was removed
I became aware of your shortcomings
Such undesirable traits
I began to dislike you
Yet I loved you just the same

During my adolescence
You couldn't tell me a thing
I refused to listen
Because rebellion set in
You were always yelling and screaming
You annoyed me to no end
And yet still I loved you

As a young adult I've endured much heartache
Your treatment of me caused me to sometimes wonder
If you loved me
Despite my confusion
I still loved you

The treatment to which I was subjected
It took years for me to see past
My state of confusion is long gone
And I realize at last
Becoming an adult has allowed me to understand
You did the best you could
If told I could choose another
I don't think that I would
My dearest mother
I love you because of who you are
Because you helped me become who I am

The Intimacy I Lack

He stole my innocence
Abused my trust
Left me filled with prudence
Inflated with disgust
As I vowed never to allow myself to be hurt again

He told me to keep our secret
Despite my shame
He said no one would believe me
How could they ignore a child in so much pain
Then I vowed never to allow myself to be hurt again

I wanted to tell
Each time he came near
At the top of my lungs just yell
But I would always succumb to my fear
Since I didn't think anyone would hear
I didn't want to be blamed
For what was happening to me
Or deal with accusations of being insincere
And I vowed never to allow myself to be hurt again

The violations became more frequent
As his power over my mind grew
And each occurrence was more severe
I wished that someone else knew
The suffering I was going through
Then came that horrible night

Gone was my will to fight
And I sat there staring into space
With tears streaming down my face
As he stared at me
Simple molestation brought him frustration
He wanted more
No one could help me now
I couldn't believe what I was about to allow
He had won this chase
And the crime he committed would scar me for life
My existence consumed with strife
Completely erasing the desire to be touched by a male
So I vowed never to allow myself to be hurt again

The intimacy I lack
Will I ever get it back

On The Other Side of the Door...

But She Didn't Scream

It was a familiar face on the other side of the door
A family friend who had spent many nights in her home
Why shouldn't she let him in
She didn't know what he was anxiously seeking
He had been busy in the streets looking for acceptance
Someone
Anyone
Help to ease the pain from his girlfriend's departure
No idea of the path his life would travel
Befriended by a stranger
Given the opportunity to experience momentary bliss
Unaware of the powerful development
On the other side of the door

Overtaken by his overwhelming addiction
Jobless and destitute
Deserted by family with nowhere to turn
He headed to her house for money to feed his acquired need
Armed
Dangerous
Deranged
Ringing her doorbell
On the other side of the door

Expressing his need for money
Upset because she had none to offer

Acknowledging another need
Aroused by suppressed desirous feelings
Determined not to awaken the children
Forced upstairs
She didn't know what awaited her
On the other side of the door
But she didn't scream
She couldn't

Disappointing him with her lack of options
Frightened by the gun he drew
Pleading with him not to harm her or her children
Compelled to comply with his sexual demands
Desperate to survive
She left him satisfied
On the other side of the door
But she didn't scream
She wouldn't

Though he was sexually pleased
He still had another need
Calling him
He led her downstairs to call someone
Anyone who would give her money for him
They went outside and he dropped her hand
And into the house she ran
Now safe
On the other side of the door
She still didn't scream
Even though she could

It took a long time for me to understand
  That all of my ups and downs

    Make me who I am

I'm glad that a higher power is in control

  To keep me from destroying myself

    Body and soul

And So I Eat...

I'm lonely...and so I eat
I'm sad...and so I eat
I'm bored...and so I eat
I'm upset...and so I eat
I'm hungry...and so I eat
And then I eat some more
Sized-sixteen seams scream for mercy
Yet still I eat

What is the result
Mounds of extra flesh
Pounds both unwanted and not welcomed
This state of existence
The product of food and me
My closest conception
It doesn't seem to want to leave
Instead it grows at a rapid rate
Adding to my discomfort

Discomfort I have endured for years
All throughout grade school jeers from peers
Passersby become onlookers offering stares
As if I am some horrific accident they just witnessed
How rude they seem to me

I find no comfort at home
Where I am the topic of jokes
From my family members
Jokes to them
But insults to me

No one offers support for me
To end this detrimental love/hate relationship
My love of the taste of unhealthy foods at war with
My hate of the manifested results of its consumption
Lacking the discipline to eat healthy
Cursed with taste buds addicted to fatty foods
This addiction is unlike any other
Because food is necessary for life

And so I eat...
For the comfort I am unable to find within myself
The comfort that temporarily fills
My unidentifiable void

Naturally Beautiful

I was born beautiful
Beautiful naturally
My grandparents didn't think so
But I disagree
Bea Bea and Ganny Ma said I was so ugly
Thought I looked like a wet rat
Comparing your grandchild to a rodent
Imagine that
Good thing I didn't believe them
My mommie helped me see
That I was born beautiful
Beautiful naturally

My Joy

It is the first day
Only
When the motionless act of lying still
Produces inner disturbances
Permeating my abdomen
The beginning of my gift

I ache
From the depth of my loins
Lower leg muscles burn
As if I've exercised for hours
Hot coffee
Hot tea
A heating pad
I need something hot to soothe me
But only today

Tomorrow there will be no pain with this gift
One day of discomfort for this experience that I treasure

I Wear A Mask

A wave of relief overcomes me
Because exit#134 is approaching
The time to lose my mask is close at hand
No matter how many times my car turns onto the street
I never tire of those anticipatory feelings I get
Once I let up the garage door
Enter the house
Close the door
The mask immediately dissolves

Why is this so
Inquisition consumes my mind
I'm not ashamed of how I look
Who I am
Or anything I've ever done
However my desire to be a very private person
Causes me to act out a façade in public
No one but those involved and a selected few are privy
To my personal business
That's always been my philosophy
It's strange considering
People who don't know me well
Are usually the ones chosen
As participants in my personal affairs
Do I wear a mask while I'm with them
Who am I really
Does anyone know
Do I even know

Is the mask hiding me from me
What a shame that would be
I don't know why
I live this lie
Or how long I will continue to wear a mask

The Torment Within

Day after day I show up
Excited about the ideas
I've spent hours pondering over
Will they embrace them
Reject them
Ridicule them
I never know
One spotlight appears to let me know that
Not only are the ideas embraceable
But capable of expansion as well
Shine light shine
For all to see
Allow your glow to send rays of warmth
To the cold bodies surrounding you
Keep them from forcing you
To become a shadow in the background
Please don't fade away into the scenery
I need you for validation
The hope that my efforts are not in vain

South Beach Soirée

Skin everywhere
More flesh than one has ever seen
And so people join in
When in Rome do as the Romans
And so people do
Drinking in the hotel until senseless
Then walking the strip scantily clothed
Looking for one night stands
One night stands looking for victims
Clubbing still in search of the one
With whom you'll spend one night
Drinking more to impair one's vision
Lowering standards to increase one's choices
Making a choice
Choosing a place
To meet up
And do the deed
The one that will never be mentioned again
South Beach
Sin city of the south
I've been there

So Much To Write, So Little Time

Writing is therapeutic
Or so I've been told
It gives me the chance to bear my soul
To cleanse my mind of deep thoughts
So much to write
So little time

I become consumed
Words seem to be everywhere
In my mind like a child's room cluttered with toys
Where is the paper when I need it
So much to write
So little time

Written language is so fascinating to me
My mind is the air after a factory explosion
My thoughts are the pollution
Sleep evades me and I must comply
So much to write
So little time

Enclosing Walls

Time alone exists no more
Since I moved here
Someone is always around
Before
I lived alone
Alone was good
No one to answer to
No one to monitor my actions
And make unwanted comments
I try closing the door to the room I occupy
In search of some privacy
But I end up feeling like a gerbil
Only I have no wheel to work out my frustration
This compares to taking an animal from the forest
And caging it in a zoo
Removing it from its natural habitat
Requiring it to adjust to a new environment
My home was my comfort zone
Now I sit here in this space
Where the walls are closing in on me

My Drug Of Choice

Personal matters begin to dissipate as I enter the room
Enveloped in the chaos I thrive to survive
Each challenge embraces me
Forcing me to find a way out
Options, options, options…
I need more options
The expectations are innumerable
Often with both hands tied behind my back
Legs bound and mouth gagged
Eyes covered with a blindfold
I am expected to perform miracles
Who has time to focus on personal matters
I have experienced the longest state of euphoria
I could have ever imagined
No harm no foul
Because in this state I can help people
Who will go on to help other people
What a marvelous domino effect I have encountered
I wish more people would get hooked on my drug of choice
The classroom

Without The Lights

At the most inopportune hour
She disconnected your power
And left us in the dark

No air conditioner to combat the humid atmosphere
We were in for some discomfort
That much was clear
At least we could open the windows for a summer breeze
Instead of walking around in the winter about to freeze
After soaking by candlelight in a tub of cool water
We felt relieved
And we walked around naked
Just you and me together
Without the lights

The food began to spoil
Because we forgot to empty the refrigerator
The disgusting stench that filled the air
Made us want to get out of there
At least we were on the second floor
So we could open the balcony door
With no fear of nosy neighbors watching
As we walked around naked
Just you and me together
Without the lights

After shampooing my hair
You sat across the room from me in your favorite chair
As I struggled to redo my double strand twists
Watching in silence you wondered
How I managed with no mirror and in the dark
As we sat around naked
Just you and me together
Without the lights

Later the outside temperature had fallen
Darkness spread throughout the sky
With our candles nearly burned out
I was about to say goodbye
Until you convinced me to stay
You wanted my company
You needed my company
That night we slept naked
Just you and me together
Without the lights

Sentimental Space

I had just begun to look around my space
No one had been here in a while
The reconstruction had begun
And I was beginning to appreciate its potential
Anxiously awaiting the renovation to be done
My mind travels back in time as
Memories invade my space
Some good
Others not so good
I wonder why I haven't replaced that revolving door
I can't imagine what possessed me to put it there before
I should have gotten rid of it long ago

My sentimental space

I never thought it could be repaired
So much damage
My vow is to be more careful
In choosing the occupants
Many people don't respect your space
They don't treat it properly
Their presence leaves scratches and dents
Prompting the need for it to heal
Soon it begins to lose its appeal
It then becomes time for a fire drill
Everyone out
Only this time no one is allowed back in
Until you can figure out where to begin

The repair that is necessary to initiate
Your healing process
Your space has been disfigured
By someone who didn't realize its value
But soon you'll make it through
As a survivor

There are times

When you cross paths

With someone

Who sets your heart on fire

But unfortunately

Their departure

Only leaves you

With overwhelming desire

This Empty Bed We Share

In the beginning expressing our love was a daily affair
Incredibly irresistible intimacy
Much deeper than just intercourse
Most times I would bury my head in your chest
And you would just hold me
To make me feel safe
Enjoying one another's company
Lying in silence
Occasionally we glared into each other's eyes
Holding hands
In the absence of words
We said everything that needed to be said

The space between us grew
No longer did we spoon until we fell asleep
Instead we claimed sides
You were on the right with me on the left
Nothing in the middle to draw us together

Our bed...
Was once filled with passion
Overflowed with love
Always welcomed us both
Yielded pleasant emotions
But with time has grown cold

Like being alone in a crowded room
Where the people can't hear me
Because to them I am invisible
I am alone with you in our bed
I can still look over and see you
But it's as if you aren't there
I miss your body next to mine
The way we intertwined our legs
Your toenails gently scratching me
While I tried to warm up your freezing feet

Our bodies now like the seashells that occupy the beach
Lie in wait for someone to show interest
What happened to the interest we had in each other

Our bed now devoid of tender loving care
Where we have no time or attention for each other
Has become this empty bed we share

I Needed You To Need Me...Completely

Your emotional absence cut me to the core
No pain I had ever experienced was comparable
So much to do
You always had so much to do
Where was my time
Reality set in
I no longer fit in
To your schedule of events
But you still loved me
So you said
I needed you to need me
Completely

Never once did I have to question your fidelity
You were by far the most faithful man I'd ever known
You always had time for our physical encounters
And I was grateful for that part
You satisfied my body with no uncertainty
But what about my mind and heart
You were perfectly content with our arrangement
Quality time was not desirable to you
And you still loved me
So you said
I needed you to need me
Completely

The Pain You Bring

You speak and I ache
Your voice mirrors the sound of a whistle being blown
No
Fingernails scratching a chalkboard
Why does your presence pain me so
I just want to escape
Away from you
But when you're not around me I feel blue
Each time I ask you to take me out
You refuse
Why do you insist on making me feel so used
You have the money
And I don't think it's funny
That you won't treat me like the lady that I am
You have no problem hanging out
Spending time and money with your boys
Taking trips out of town
If you want me physically
Then you come around
2AM calls soliciting my sex
Where were you earlier tonight
The time may have been right
To have your needs met
Mine, too, for that matter
What you need is an ever ready mattress
With a hole in the middle
It's not some kind of riddle
I'm fed up

Something about you seems corrupt
Are you simply unwilling to commit
If so, then I quit
Your lack of care
Gives me feelings of despair
About this relationship
I know I've said goodbye before
But behind me this time please lock the door
I have no intention of returning anymore
I don't need the pain you bring
I don't need you for anything

When He Doesn't Want To Come Home

What do you do
When he doesn't want to come home

You cooked
You cleaned
You paid the bills
You took care of all of the children's needs
But he still doesn't want to come home

You begged
You pleaded
Sacrificed yourself
To give him everything he needed
There was nothing you wouldn't do
To make even his wildest dreams come true
But he still doesn't want to come home

He's so far away
Emotionally untouchable
Your every contact is mechanic
He comes to give you money
Or just to see the kids
He shows no love for you
He has no conversation
You long for an embrace
His thoughts are not there with you
They're in some distant place
Because he doesn't want to come home

Sometimes he looks right through you
Like you're not even there
Your efforts to get his attention are in vain
No bubble bath or sweet perfume
No lingerie you wear
Can stop him from causing you all of this pain
Because he doesn't want to come home

Your mind is boggled with conflicting thoughts
There has to be someone else
Though you can't be sure
You plot and scheme to win him back
Your kids need their dad
You want your husband
You need your family in tact
But he still doesn't want to come home

Your frustration level
Has soared to a new height
You've tried everything you know

What do you do
When he doesn't want to come home
Exhale a breath and let go

I Still Want You

Why are we apart
When I still want you
Yesterday I saw you across a crowded room
Talking with others
Laughing
You looked so happy
How can you be happy without me
What about me
I want to be happy, too
I know I ended the relationship
But you know that I still want you

These past three months have been extremely hard
I've cried myself to sleep every night
You've occupied all of my dreams
I can't get you out of my sight
Each day my first thought is of you it seems
It's true
Because I still want you

At my birthday party I fell apart
Sitting there crying at my mom's dining room table
She sat there helpless
Watching a child she loved
Hurt so deeply inside
Why won't I let go of my pride
And ask you to come home
When I know that I still want you

My sister saw you at the movie theatre
With your new girl and her kids
I can't understand why you seem totally unfazed
While I'm on autopilot walking around dazed
You're already playing house with someone new
Even though you know that I still want you

Missing you tremendously
I broke the rule and called
You said you were glad to hear from me
I had been on your mind
Said you had to see me

As soon as you entered the door
My feelings came rushing back
Like tidal waves hitting the shore
You held me tight
I held you tighter
I wanted you even more
Than I ever had before

Then we made love
And I began to cry
Tears of joy and pain

You said you couldn't stay
How can you stay away
When you know that I still want you

My Fixation

So much time has passed, since you left
But every morning when I wake up
I still see your face
Even though you're not really there
I have fallen in love with you
Without being aware
I can't believe how deep
My fondness for you has grown
How could I have known
That meeting you would change my outlook on life
The walls of my heart were penetrated
My mind was concentrated
Like a scientific solution in a chemistry class
My heart's core was an element
Combined with desire for you
Transformed into a compound
Whenever you came around
I experienced complete infiltration
No wonder I felt like a high school girl
And when you went away
I felt an earthquake hit my world
With no clue of what to do
Especially since I could no longer have you
The night you left was filled with gloom
Alone in the dark in the center of the room
My mind replayed many of our precious moments
And even some of our spats
I was willing to do anything to get you back

As I cried in a manner that was uncontrollable

For me there was no consolation

I only wanted you

My fixation

Someone for me to love

There may never be another

So when will I recover

As I Wait For Your Return

Anticipation controls my mind
And I begin to wonder
About the enormous amount of time
Before I see you again

How vivid the memory of the day you left
You were insistent that we didn't say goodbye
I lost the battle of fighting back my tears
And I began to cry

So you held me
Tighter than you had ever held me before
You had to be strong enough for both of us
Otherwise you couldn't have walked out of the door

Everyday I kiss your picture
Your promise to return is what keeps me holding on
My desire to hear your voice increases
As I count the hours that you've been gone
My emotional void runs very deep
And nothing else can fill it
Sometimes I struggle finding sleep
So all night I just sit
Looking at old photographs
Taking trips down memory lane
Reminiscing about moments we've shared
Some happy
Some challenging

And how we always made it through
Just me and you
I wish you could be here with me now
To never let you go would be my vow

Though I understand that you can't
It still doesn't help me when I yearn
To feel your warm embrace
As I wait for your return
I envision your beautiful face
And focus on our memories
That cannot be replaced

For A Short Time My Love

The day we met
Was one I'll never forget
For I knew that I had found a friend
Spending moments with you for only a short time
Has been worth this heartache I'm now enduring
I'd known since the beginning
You would have to leave
Eliminating any need for me to grieve
For I can now say
I know what it is like to be rich
To me you are a treasure
Far beyond measure
And no one could understand
What it was like to have you as mine
Even for a short time
You met all of my needs
And left me with endless memories
Of our time together
To keep me smiling
Even though you're no longer here
You're in my heart
So you'll always be near
My love

Unforgettable Goodbye

I looked over my shoulder
And there you were
Standing behind me
Nameless
Faceless
Making me weak in the knees with your touch
Orgasmic desires inflating my insides
I wondered who you were
Why did you have this effect on me
You slithered into my heart
Like a snake
Emitting your venomous liquid
It was more than I could take
Too much of your poisonous potion
Dispelled the notion
That I would ever again be in control of my emotions
Thoughts of you
Occupied my mind constantly
I began committing acts I said I wouldn't
And I displayed behavior I knew I shouldn't
I no longer recognized myself
All of my values and morals placed on a shelf
Of all the books
Buried deep behind
Too well hidden for me to find
What was I to do
Since I had given all of my power to you
Who would I turn to

For help to come through
The darkness of this tunnel
Blind
That's what I had become
No longer traveling by sight
Having loss all of my might
Lacking the strength to fight
I needed someone to save me
My life now void of harmony
The temporary pleasure was no longer worth it
We both needed to quit
Despite my addiction to your wit
The situation was now too complicated
So you were forced to say goodbye
And though sadness consumed me
I refused to cry
Because overshadowing the negative
Are precious moments
That will live on in my heart forever

Breaking the Cycle…A Letter to My Love

What is it about you
That has me so confused
I know what I want to do
And you know my stubbornness
My mind is unequivocally made up
Until you speak
You have this indescribable effect on me
Why can't I just say no to you

Sometimes you make me so sick
Literally
I can vaguely tell who I am
When you come around
All of my strength and defenses
Zapped
In one instant you render me powerless
Making it difficult to refuse your requests

So I just sit often times and wait
For sensible thoughts to circulate
Throughout my mind so that I can contemplate
Whether or not I belong
In this cyclical situation we call a relationship

We once had an incident
And I accept full responsibility for my bad judgment
I watched your shell walk around
6'3" tall and 190 beautiful pounds

Clean shaven head
Broad shoulders and washboard abs
With the most attractive feet I've ever seen on a male
Even your toenails look good
So strong in appearance
Yet carrying around all of that pain
Aching and being eaten away at the center
Like an uneaten, shiny, red apple with a worm at the core

Though it didn't seem like it to you
I was hurting, too
I cried until there were no tears left to fall
I had isolated my friends
So there was no one I could call
No moisture or residue in the wells of my eyes
Guilt ridden feelings that refused to compromise
I needed you to forgive me
More importantly, I needed to forgive myself
So I tried to run away

Throughout it all you maintain a huge presence in my life
No matter how many times I try to break free
I free my body
But my heart remains
From around my heart, I loosen the chains
But my mind continues to be shackled

It makes me wonder if you really love me
Or if you just don't want me to be loved by someone else
It seems challenging for you to decide
I wish you wouldn't operate on foolish pride

This is not a game
It's my life
Find a way to give me the love that I need
Or find the compassion to set me free
Seriously

Infidelity...

It's been said that

Love has no rhyme and no

reason

Yielding to uncontrollable urges

That lasts for a season

Be careful

About hurting those that love

you

The Forbidden Love

I wonder what you see
When you look at me
When I look at you
I see through you
Beyond the shell that houses your soul
And I surrender control
But only to you

No need to look deep into your eyes
Each conversation draws me further in
To the web you spin
It's not a web of lies
Nor of deceit
It makes being captured
Oh so sweet
Like the honey left by bees
You hit the target
As you aim to please

Our connection is deeper than physical
You stimulate my mind
You satisfy my body
You gratify my soul
You deal with the whole
Person that I am
I welcome your honesty
No hidden agendas
It inspires me to be free

Just as you reveal yourself to me
I can be around you without being judged
Standing naked before you
With no fear of you pointing out a smudge
Because you accept me
And just let me be

When I have nothing to say at all
You still want me to call
Until I find the words to speak
Then you listen intently to whatever I need to say
I can tell you anything
You should be my king
But you aren't
Because you belong to someone else
I can't keep you for myself

How did we get into this state
It shouldn't be anyone's fate
To be miserable
But we have no choice

And Then You Left

You befriended me when no one else would
At first I resisted
But your smile was inviting
Hypnotic
Your persistence
Soon overpowered my resistance

Before long most of our time was spent together
Whether on the telephone or in person
Minutes became hours
Hours grew to days
Resulting in many steamy nights

Not only had you captured my heart
You reached the depths of my soul
Unlike any other person I had ever known
In my mind no one else could come close

One day I awakened to discover
That I had fallen in love with you
Then the tables began to turn
Your time for me underwent metamorphosis
From abundant to nearly nonexistent
Hooked on a drug I couldn't have
I became hopeless
You spoiled me
And then you left

It Was Then That I Left

Your absence was not physical
You never failed in that department
Far worse than that
It was emotional
And it left a deep void
In my struggle through withdrawal
I was drawn to another person
I used him to treat the condition that had developed
He represented comfort
Something was familiar about this scene
Before long most of our time was spent together
Whether on the telephone or in person
Minutes became hours
Hours grew to days
Up close and personal
He rejuvenated my emotions
From their state of dormancy
I began to desire him
It was then that I left

But You Wouldn't Let Go

Both emotionally and physically
I abandoned the relationship you and I had built
In my mind

We still talked daily
But I was long gone
With our suspended physical relationship
Your suspicion grew
I could no longer avoid your attempts to seduce me
I had to end the relationship
To refrain from hurting you
Anymore than I already had
But you wouldn't let go

Your mouth said OK
You even gave back my car and door keys
But you wouldn't let go

You called and called
Pressuring me for an explanation
Is it another man
Is it another man
Over and over again
You questioned me
My efforts to protect your feelings
Were yielding to
The desire to relieve my feelings of guilt
And so I did it
I confessed
But you still wouldn't let go

I Should Leave You Alone...

I should leave you alone...
Because you've had more than enough time to choose
Because she is your wife
Because we both have so much to lose
Because you made a vow for life

I should leave you alone...
Because you've been dishonest
Because you have a family
Because you keep breaking promises
Because you really don't deserve me

I should leave you alone...
Because our relationship is doomed to fail
Because whenever we're out you continue to flirt
Because of all the lies you tell
Because innocent people are being hurt

I should leave you alone...
Before this situation hits the fan
But I just can't seem to break free
What's worse is that I can't understand
Exactly what's wrong with me

I should leave you alone...
And take back control of my life
I must come back to reality
Like the vow you made to your wife
I'm making a vow to love me

The Day I Brought You Flowers

As I entered the door I could not contain
The joy I felt within
Spread ear to ear was my grin
With card in hand
I looked around
To me you were in demand
The star of this show
And you didn't even know
I was there
The shower was going
I saw the steam
I wanted to join in
But I knew you liked the water too hot for me
So I waited outside the door on your bed
Excited to share my gift
I drifted off reminiscing about last night
Then I heard the voice that still echoes in my mind
Imagine my fright
Who was in the shower
Talking with you
Laughing
About just finishing an unmentionable act
How could I be so naïve
These flowers you will never receive
You rushed me out of the house this morning
Without so much as a kiss goodbye
But I was so happy about last night
I didn't even bother to ask why

Now I know

Your next engagement would be coming soon

And you couldn't have me in the way

What a fool I've been

Never again

At least not for you

The day I brought you flowers

Had me sobbing tears for hours

What an eye opener for me

Though my heart is aching, I will love again

You'll see

Infidelity

Adultery and lies
Hand and glove
For so called love
Our scent of deceit infuses the sheets
I'm looking at you lying in my bed
While lying on the telephone to your wife
When did this become my life
I've dreamed of a future with you
One that can never be
The unfathomable concept of you, her, and me
How can we escape
This state of infidelity

Your Passage

You entered my life
Like the force of a storm
With torrential rains
And powerful winds
In complete control
As if you belonged here

Initially I was hesitant
My heart like the sun
Peeking from behind the clouds
Unsure if it should come out and bear itself to you
But you lured it out
With promises to always be true

The rain dried up
The winds had ceased
I welcomed the brightly lit sun
Shining on me
Warming me inside and out

Knowing you felt good
Talking to you felt better
Being with you was the best
And I was craving you
At first

Unaware of your tortuous plan
Manipulative
Deceptive
Exposing me to unbelievable sorrow
You had ill intentions from the very start
And I know that I had to play my part
But why did you choose me

Strange calls began
False accusations
Excuses
You had so many
Insincere apologies
Of them you had plenty
Bloating my stomach
Intestinal waste
That had to be passed
At last

Our Relationship's Demise

Our relationship was perfect
In my mind
There was nothing I wouldn't have done for you

I was working two jobs
Keeping house and loving you
With every ounce of my being
You shouldn't have wanted for anything
Yet you still weren't satisfied
Only I didn't know
Why didn't you tell me what you needed from me

While I was at work, you were running the streets
But I never complained
Even when you were late picking me up
I still never questioned you
You did what you wanted to do
As long as you were home at night with me
I was as happy as I could be

Then came the day I kept the car
I wanted to be early picking you up from work
Man did you make me look like a jerk
Standing outside with her sharing a smoke
Sharing a smoke, what a joke

You said it was nothing, that she was no one
Unbeknownst to me, you were playing 'dad' to her son
It was with her and him where
You were spending all of your time
But she was no one
What a line

Slowly but surely
She was taking my place
I didn't even have a chance to plead my case
Because you convinced me that I was overreacting
I had nothing to worry about
You kept saying it was nothing
She was no one

Then you did the ultimate
You had her at our place
Forget knife in the back
That was a slap in the face
I'm working hard—all about paying the bills
You're entertaining her in our home
Not even thinking about how I feel
How could you do that to me

Enough was enough
I finally broke down
I could no longer bear to have you around
So I asked you to leave

I couldn't believe you tried to blame me
Asking who did I meet
And why was I cheating
Your violent reaction had me extremely afraid
You'd never hit me before
But suddenly you'd changed
I knew we were over
There was no turning back
Especially after the physical attack

Next to me that night, like a baby you slept
While curled in the fetal position, like a baby I wept
Unsure if you'd awaken to hurt me again
Yet certain our relationship had come to an end

At last morning arrived so that you could leave
Alone in what was once our home
I could finally grieve
I was in so much pain; it was unbelievable
The thought of living without you was inconceivable
I needed strength to go on, and to dry my tired eyes
Because I had to accept our relationship's demise

I'm Sorry, And What?

Two simple words
With very little weight
Extremely overused
In an effort to communicate

Communicate what...
One's sincere regret
For a misspoken word
An inconsiderate action
Or thought misheard

To your I'm sorry
I say, "And what?"

Saying I'm sorry doesn't...
Erase the pain
Ease the bad feeling
Eliminate the shame
Expedite the healing

The words I'm sorry are exactly how they sound
SORRY
All too often people believe
That saying those two words clears the slate
An effect to their cause is hard for them to conceive
Yet they find it easy to speculate
That you'll be just fine
After hearing those two words

Such a thought is asinine
Completely absurd

To your I'm sorry
I say, "And what?"

A parent misses a recital or a baseball game
A lover forgets a special day or calls out the wrong name
Disappointment arrives and settles deeply within
Those two overused, simple words
Don't even know where to begin
To crack the surface
Tackle the hurt
And make everything okay
Yet they're spoken
Over and over again
Almost everyday

To your I'm sorry
I say, "And what?"

Tell me something
That I find comforting
To ease my bad feeling
To expedite my healing
What are you going to do
How are things going to change

Can you make sure I never feel this pain again
Can you make sure I never experience this shame again
Tell me how you're going to make me anew
I can't take it if things stay the same

Only then will I realize
That you honestly apologize
To your I'm sorry
I won't have to ask, 'and what?'
Because I'll know for sure
That you'll make a conscious effort
Never to hurt me anymore

Suffering a loss...

Some circumstances

Tug at your heart strings

Always remember

The joy that compassion brings

With A Heavy Heart

It's been three years now
Sadness sometimes envelopes my mind
And I'm momentarily incapacitated
I no longer ask why

I now realize
That it was just her time to go
Away from all of her family
And friends who loved her so

I told her mom I'd keep in touch
I know that I should call
It's hard just thinking about it
But there's no excuse at all
I talked to her with ease when my TRU was here
Now our conversations make the truth clear
She's lost a child who will never be replaced
And I've lost my one TRU friend
No other best friend will I seek
Rather than make each other strong
I think we make each other weak
Reality shines a flashlight on your grief
It spotlights emotions you try to hide
Deep inside

One day I was relaxing and enjoying my personal space
Then my TRU's daughter called
And though she sounded upbeat
Her voice sent my spirits into a dark place
It's amazing how resilient children can be
While adults walk around in denial or disbelief

At times I thought I couldn't make it
I'd be in so much pain
And I would bellow a guttural moan
Sounding as if I were insane
I simply couldn't understand
Why she would leave me alone

I finally discovered that it wasn't about me
My maker had decided to set her free
From all the worldly cares that stressed her so
I knew if she had a choice, she wouldn't want to go
And though we are now worlds apart
My life can go on even with a heavy heart

Yesterday I Called My TRU

Nineteen months
That's how long it's been
Since I dialed her number
I didn't even know that I still remembered it
Deep thoughts of her penetrated my mind
As I rode the train home
I still miss her
Sometimes

I pulled out my cell phone to call someone
I can't remember who it was
My subconscious was in control
My finger dialed her number
As if it had a mind of its own
There they were
On my screen
Those familiar numbers
The ten digits I so often dialed to speak with her
I realized it
When I checked to see if the call had connected
The levy holding a floodgate of emotions
Was steadily wavering
Then I did it
I pushed send
Still in a fog
I wondered
Who would answer
My TRU's number

What would I say when they answered
How could I justify dialing her number
When she's been gone almost two years
I waited
And listened
The piercing shrill of a fax machine
Jolted me out of the haze
At least no one else would answer my TRU's number
This time
To remind me that she's gone
As I hung up my mind
Became a digital camera frozen in time
Snapshots of happy moments we spent together
My twenty-one year friendship is no more

I remember her talking of us growing old together
But that will never be
Without her I must still grow old
The thought alone makes me feel cold
She's not coming back, and I realize
I still miss her
Sometimes

Some situations in life

Cause people to be consumed with strife

When one's will to live is almost lost

Encourage survival at all costs

My Humble Existence

not even considered a Meager individual
my Meaningless existence
in this Mindless world
has become Mortifying

day after day i Search
for Shelter
from the Storms i encounter
receiving Scowls because of my appearance
being Shunned because of my predicament

Desertion by my family
Diminished my will to try
now i am Desolate
my spirit is Destroyed
and not because i was on Drugs
merely consumed with Despair

i had hopes and dreams Once
before i was Ostracized by society
Oblivious to this state in which i have found myself
previously unwilling to help One person in need
i now sit in daily Observation
wondering if anyone will Offer to help me

Stop The Violence

That husband who beats his wife
The mother who abuses her child
One stranger who attacks another
Actions like animals in the wild
Why is there so much violence

This girl wants to fight over he say/she say rumors
Those boys want to fight over the same
Children are fighting their parents
All of us are to blame
Why is there so much violence

Looks become stares filled with hate
Comments lead to insults
Such an awful way to communicate
Almost always yielding undesirable results
Why is there so much violence

Words of anger
Become daggers spawn from the tongue
Piercing the hearts of many a soul
No consideration for the feelings of others
Like the inside of a freezer, people can be so cold
Why is there so much violence

Raging emotions
Fists swarming like bees
Bites, bruises, broken bones
Injuries hard to believe
Why is there so much violence

Intelligent humans are superior to animals
We have hearts filled with compassion to share
Yet animals seem to know how to get along better
When will we learn to love each other
And show how much we care
Why is there so much violence

STOP THE VIOLENCE!

My Addiction

His presence in my life
Was comparable to cancer
Malignant
Invading the systems of my body
Like a *malediction*

His words
Polluting the recesses
Of my brain
Suffocating my mind
With *male*volent thoughts

His *male*fic actions
Puncturing the inner chambers of my heart
Inconceivable incapacitating internal incisions
Wounds even the most skilled surgeon could not reach

This *male*ficent person
The worst *male*factor
I had ever known
Or would ever know
Male

In all of your relationships…
Keep the lines of communication

Clear

To Rhyme or Not to Rhyme...

**M
E
S
S
A
G
E
S**

of the Heart

About the author

AnGenette is an educator with a passion for both spoken and written word. She has spent the last eight years teaching and learning from many diverse groups of students throughout the greater Atlanta area. Last year, while teaching a poetry unit, she had the pleasure of being exposed to an enormous amount of student talent. This experience served as the catalyst she needed to finally complete her personal poetry project. AnGenette is currently on hiatus, but anxiously anticipating her return to the field of education.

Contact Information

AnGenette D. Jackson

Post Office Box 1308

Lithonia, GA 30058

aj.the.writer@hotmail.com

www.ingramcontent.com/pod-product-compliance
Lightning Source LLC
Chambersburg PA
CBHW020312290526
45784CB00003B/1475